Winter

It is winter.

The tree has no leaves.
Where have the leaves gone?

The leaves have blown away.
They will grow back in spring.

The pond has no ducks.
Where have the ducks gone?

The ducks have flown away to a warm place.
They will come back in spring.

The park has no squirrels.
Where have the squirrels gone?

The squirrels have hidden away in a warm place.
They will come back in spring.

The garden has no flowers.
Where have the flowers gone?

The bulbs are in the ground.
They will grow back in spring.

The nest has no chicks.
Where have the chicks gone?

The chicks have grown and flown away to a warm place. They will come back in spring.

The park has no butterflies.
Where have the butterflies gone?

The butterflies have flown away to a warm place.
They will come back in spring.

The playground has no children.
Where have the children gone?

The children are at home.
They are waiting for
the warm spring weather, too!